Dedication

For Raghu, Manu, Gopu and Madhav.
And all the great kids of the world.

You are what you believe in. You become what you believe you can become...
Bhagavad Gita

Namaste and Hello. My name is Diya. I am 6 years old.

I live in New Delhi, the capital of India.

Meet my parents. My mummy likes wearing a saree and papa likes wearing the kurta-pajama.

My mummy takes me to school every day in an auto-rickshaw.

I call it tuk-tuk. The tuk-tuk has three wheels.

At school we learn lots of things.

I love to play with my friends and cousins.

Do you know the name of the game I am playing?

3
5
6
8
7

I love animals!

At the zoo, I like to ride the elephant. He is called Raju.

There are lots of elephants in India.

Would you like to ride an elephant?

We love cows because they give us milk to drink.

I like feeding the cow.

She is very sweet and gentle.

I went to visit the Red Fort in Old Delhi with my mummy.

It is made of red stone.

Can you see the Indian flag on top of the Red Fort?

Which colours can you see?

Every Saturday, we go to the temple to pray.

My favourite God is Lord Krishna.

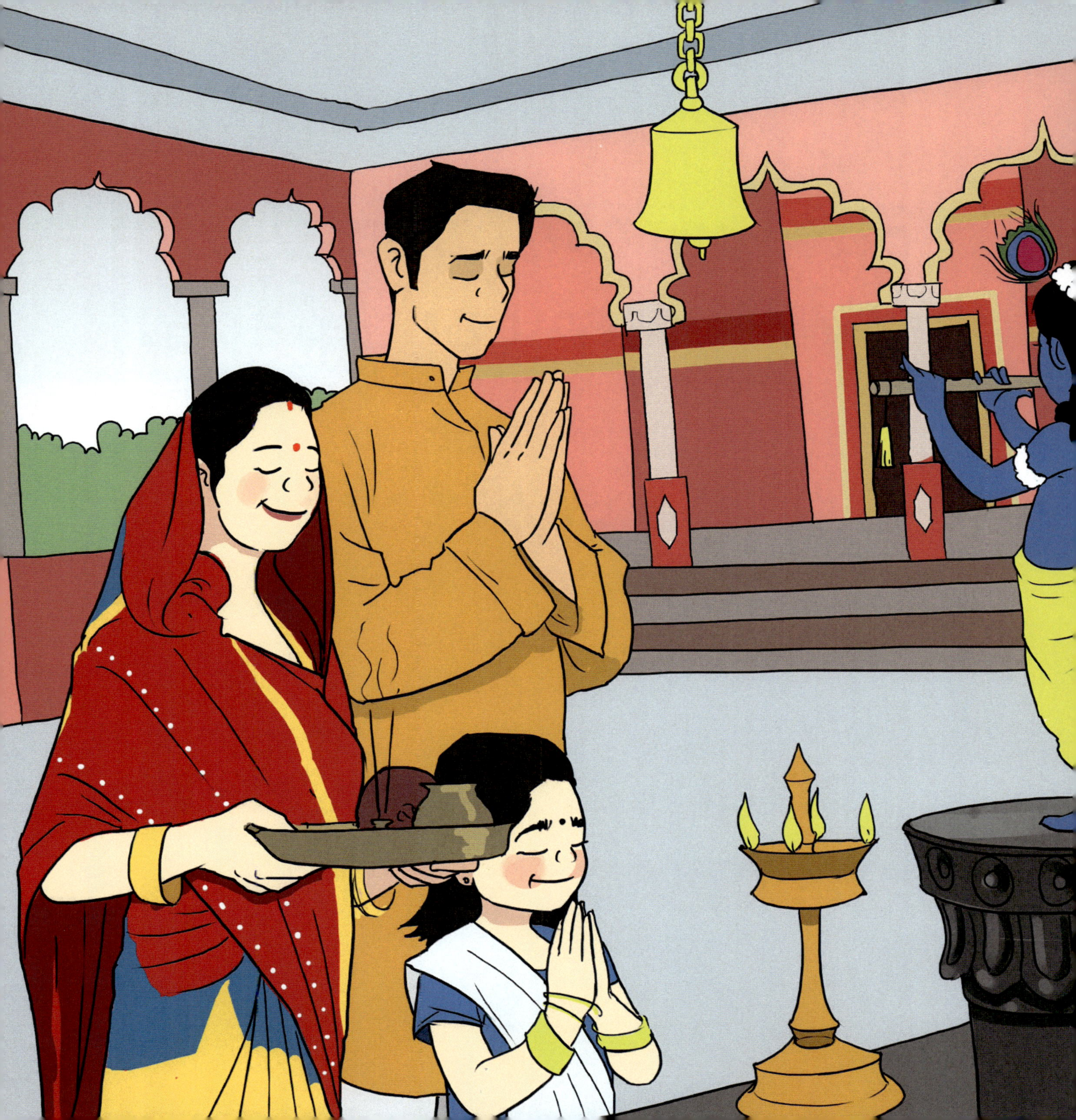

I play carrom board with my mummy and papa.

It is like a pool table. Four people can play this game.

Carrom board is very popular in India.

I like doing yoga. It calms my mind.

My favourite posture is the lotus position.

Have you tried sitting in the lotus position?

Every year we celebrate the Holi festival to welcome the spring season.

Holi is the festival of colours. We pour colours on each other.

It is also celebrated to mark the victory of good over evil.

I am learning to play the sitar.

The sitar is one of the traditional musical instruments of India.

I call my sitar teacher Guru ji.

For dinner, I eat chapattis, rice, lentils and vegetables.

I love my mummy's cooking.

I am a vegetarian.

What food do you like eating?

I drink milk before I go to sleep. My mummy reads me stories.

My favourite story is about the tiger called Sheru. Tiger is the national animal of India. Which animal do you like?

Goodnight and Namaste.

Words to learn

Namaste - Na-mas-tay

Kurta - Kur-ta

Raju - Raa-ju

Krishna - Krish-na

Carrom - Kar-rom

Holi- Ho-lee

Sitar- See-tar

Chapattis - Chap-pa-ti

Sheru - Sher-roo

Hope you have liked this book. Feel free to contact me on

info@shalusharma.com

Please visit my website for more books

https://www.amazon.com/author/shalusharma

Made in the USA
Middletown, DE
15 April 2020

89215032R00018